It is Spring.

Daddy Billy Goat,
Brother Billy Goat and
Baby Billy Goat are hungry.

Baby Billy Goat sees some tall, green grass.
'Let's eat it now,' he says.

'I'm the third
Billy Goat.
I can see the green
grass,' Baby Billy Goat says.

4

'Oh, who are you?' Baby Billy Goat says.
'I'm the troll and I'm hungry.'

'I like eating goats.'

'You're b...b...b...big. I'm small.
Please, don't eat me, I'm a baby.'

'Go on,' the troll says, 'I like big goats.'

'Mmmmm, grass,' Baby Billy Goat says.

'I'm the second Billy Goat.
I can see the green grass,'
Brother Billy Goat says.

'Oh, who are you?'
Brother Billy Goat says.
'You're b...b...b...big. I'm small.'

'I'm the troll and I'm hungry.
I like goats for lunch.'

'Please, don't eat me, I'm thin.'

'Go on,' the troll says.
'I like fat goats.'

'I'm happy!' says
Brother Billy Goat.

'I'm the first Billy Goat. I can see the green grass,' Daddy Billy Goat says.

'Grass?' said the troll.
'Grrrrrr, I like big, fat goats.
You're fat and I'm hungry.'

'And I'm strong,'
Daddy Billy
Goat says.
He throws the troll
into the water.

Daddy Billy Goat
Brother Billy Goat and
Baby Billy Goat
Eat…and eat…the grass!

Activities

Before you read

1. Can you name the animal? Draw
a line from the picture to the right word.

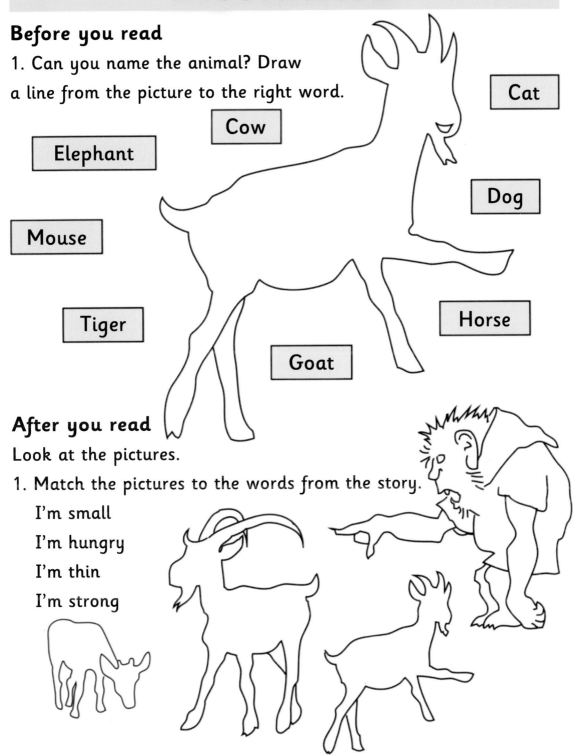

Cat

Cow

Elephant

Dog

Mouse

Tiger

Horse

Goat

After you read

Look at the pictures.

1. Match the pictures to the words from the story.

I'm small

I'm hungry

I'm thin

I'm strong

Pearson Education Limited
Pearson
KAO Two
KAO Park
Harlow
Essex
CM17 9NA

and Associated Companies throughout the world.

ISBN 9781292239972

First published by Librairie du Liban Publishers, 1996
This adaptation first published by
Penguin Books 2000
5 7 9 10 8 6
Text copyright © Pearson Education Limited 2000
Illustrations copyright © 1996 Librairie du Liban

Retold by Melanie Williams
Series Editor: Melanie Williams
The Three Billy Goats Gruff, Level 1
Illustrations by Angus McBride
Design by Neil Alexander, Monster Design

Printed in China
SWTC/05

Published by Pearson Education Limited

For a complete list of titles available in the Pearson Story Readers series please
write to your local Pearson Education office or contact:
Pearson, KAO Two, KAO Park, Harlow, Essex, CM17 9NA

Answers for the Activities in this book are published in the free Pearson English
Story Readers Factsheet on the website, www.pearsonenglishreaders.com